When It Feels Impossible to Pray

PRAYERS FOR THE GRIEVING

THOMAS MCPHERSON

PARACLETE PRESS

BREWSTER, MASSACHUSETTS

2018 First Printing
When It Feels Impossible to Pray: Prayers for the Grieving
Copyright © 2018 by Paraclete Press, Inc.
ISBN 978-1-64060-068-3

Library of Congress Cataloging-in-Publication Data
Names: McPherson, Thomas, author.
Title: When it feels impossible to pray : prayers for the grieving / Thomas
    McPherson.
Description: Brewster, Massachusetts : Paraclete Press Inc., 2017. | Includes
    index.
Identifiers: LCCN 2017050213 | ISBN 9781640600683 (trade paper)
Subjects: LCSH: Bereavement—Religious aspects—Christianity—Prayers and
    devotions. | Grief—Religious aspects—Christianity—Prayers and devotions.
Classification: LCC BV4905.3 .M36 2017 | DDC 242/.866—dc23
LC record available at https://lccn.loc.gov/2017050213

10 9 8 7 6 5 4 3 2 1

Published by Paraclete Press
Brewster, Massachusetts
www.paracletepress.com
Printed in the United States of America

CONTENTS

Openings to Prayer

YOU DON'T HAVE TO PRAY, TO PRAY. In other words, you don't have to do the things one normally associates with prayer to actually be connecting with God in a way that's prayer-like.

Just sit still if you like. Grieving people often find themselves doing a lot of sitting still. Stunned. That's perfectly fine. Just sit. Allow yourself a time to be quiet, to answer to no one, to accomplish nothing at all. Quietness in itself is prayer for many people.

Or if you're so inclined, do the opposite: get up and move. For some, sitting still at a time like this is precisely *not* what they most need. Move. Go running. Go biking. Row a boat. Swim. Walk until you are exhausted. Then, be still and listen.

There are many, many ways to pray that don't include talking, or concentrating with words, or any of those traditional postures and activities that we use at other times throughout our lives when we want to connect with God and we call that connection "prayer."

There is a classic hymn by the British Moravian James Montgomery, "Prayer Is the Soul's Sincere Desire," and the first three stanzas go like this:

Prayer is the soul's sincere desire,
uttered or unexpressed;
the motion of a hidden fire
that trembles in the breast.

Prayer is the simplest form of speech
that infant lips can try,
prayer the sublimest strains that reach
the Majesty on high.

Prayer is the Christian's vital breath,
the Christian's native air,
his watchword at the gates of death:
he enters heaven with prayer.

But there it is right there in the first two lines:

"Prayer is the soul's sincere desire, uttered or unexpressed."

You don't have to talk in order to pray.

Mother Teresa of Calcutta once said:

> We forget that in the silence of the heart God speaks,
>
> and from the fullness of the heart we speak.
>
> Only when we have heard him in the silence
>
> of our hearts, only when we have learned to listen
>
> to God in the silence of our hearts,
>
> only then can we say: I pray.

Grieving Is Godly

N O ONE NEEDS AN EXCUSE TO GRIEVE, and no one is ever prepared for what grief will mean in their lives. Grieving is not something we ever train for.

But we should realize that not only is grieving without question our right and our need, but grieving is godly.

Jesus said:

> "Blessed are those who mourn,
>
> for they will be comforted."
>
> (MATTHEW 5:4, NIV)

⌒ Jesus Grieved ⌒

In this important account from the Gospels, Jesus both comforted the grieving, and grieved himself:

> On his arrival, Jesus found that Lazarus had already been in the tomb for four days. Now Bethany was less than two miles from Jerusalem, and many Jews had come to Martha and Mary to comfort them in the loss of their brother. When Martha heard that Jesus was coming, she went out to meet him, but Mary stayed at home.
>
> "Lord," Martha said to Jesus, "if you had been here, my brother would not have died. But I know that even now God will give you whatever you ask."
>
> Jesus said to her, "Your brother will rise again."

Martha answered, "I know he will rise again in the resurrection at the last day."

Jesus said to her, "I am the resurrection and the life. The one who believes in me will live, even though they die; and whoever lives by believing in me will never die. Do you believe this?"

"Yes, Lord," she replied, "I believe that you are the Messiah, the Son of God, who is to come into the world."

After she had said this, she went back and called her sister Mary aside. "The Teacher is here," she said, "and is asking for you." When Mary heard this, she got up quickly and went to him. Now Jesus had not yet entered the village, but was still at the place where Martha had met him. When the Jews who had been with Mary in the house, comforting her, noticed how quickly she got up and went out, they followed her, supposing she was going to the tomb to mourn there.

When Mary reached the place where Jesus was and saw him, she fell at his feet and said, "Lord, if you had been here, my brother would not have died."

When Jesus saw her weeping, and the Jews who had come along with her also weeping, he was deeply moved in spirit and troubled. "Where have you laid him?" he asked.

"Come and see, Lord," they replied.

Jesus wept.

Then the Jews said, "See how he loved him!"

But some of them said, "Could not he who opened the eyes of the blind man have kept this man from dying?"

(JOHN 11:17–37, NIV)

Questions
Can Be Prayers

WHY?
Why me?
Why us?

Why was this allowed to happen?

What will happen to me now?

What is the purpose in all of this?

How am I supposed to move on?

Where will I go?

What will people think of me now?

Who am I?

Where are you, God?

Why did God do this to me?

When will I feel myself again?

When will this feeling of helplessness go away?

What's next?

16

⤚ BAD THEOLOGY ⤙
A QUIZ

A POEM BY SCOTT CAIRNS

And lo, the angel of the Lord came upon them,
and the glory of the Lord shone round about them:
and they were sore afraid.

Whenever we aver "the God is nigh,"
do we imply that He is ever otherwise?

When, in scripture, God's "anger" is said
to be aroused, just how do you take that?

If—whether now or in the fullness—we
stipulate that God is all in all, just where

or how would you position Hell? Which
is better—to break the law and soothe

the wounded neighbor, or to keep the law
and cause the neighbor pain? Do you mean it?

If another sins, what is that to you?
When the sinful suffer publicly, do you

find secret comfort in their grief, or will
you also weep? They are surely grieving;

are you weeping now? Assuming *sin* is *sin*,
whose do you condemn? Who is judge? Who

will feed the lambs? The sheep? Who, the goats?
Who will sell and give? Who will be denied?

Whose image haunts the mirror? And why
are you still here? What exactly do you hope

to become? When will you begin?

Question Prayers

There are many prayers that are more like questions than they are petitions to God or statements of faith.

> Merciful God,
>
> hear the cries of our grief,
>
> for you know the anguish of our hearts.
>
> It is beyond our understanding
>
> and more than we can bear.
>
> Accept our prayer. . . .

Out of the darkness of our grief,

we cry to you, O Lord. . . .

Lord our God,

you give and you take away.

You blessed us through the gift of *N*,

who is now taken from us

and whose loss we mourn. . . .

Eternal God and Father,

look in mercy on those who remember *N* before you.

Let not the manner of *his/her* death

cloud the good memories of *his/her* life.

Accept from us all that we feel
even when words fail. . . .

(*From* "Prayers for Those Who Mourn,"
www.churchofengland.org; adapted)

Tell the Truth

There is no timetable for your grief. You will never "get over it." Some of your questions will slowly find answers. Others will not.

The questions you have now may yield to new questions in the future. You probably want to surround yourself with people who are willing to listen to questions, and talk about them, without offering firm and definitive answers.

Listen to this:

My belief is that when you're telling the truth, you're close to God. If you say to God, "I am exhausted and depressed beyond words, and I don't like You at all right now, and I recoil from most people who believe in You," that might be the most honest thing you've ever said. If you told me you had said to God, "It is all hopeless, and I don't have a clue if You exist, but I could use a hand," it would almost bring tears to my eyes, tears of pride in you, for the courage it takes to get real—really real. It would make me want to sit next to you at the dinner table.

So prayer is our sometimes real selves trying to communicate with the Real, with Truth, with the Light. It is us reaching out to be heard, hoping to be found by a light and warmth in the world, instead of darkness and cold. Even mushrooms respond to light—I suppose they blink their mushroomy eyes, like the rest of us.

—ANNE LAMOTT, *HELP, THANKS, WOW*

You Can Ask for Hope

PERHAPS KEEP IT VERY SIMPLE TO BEGIN. God, help me. God, help us. God, help us!

Holy One, you know our fear, our dread, our anxiety, our sorrows. You promise to share these things with us. You promise to be our hope. Be it now.

I am devastated. You are here with me . . . watching . . . with me. You have been with me in the past . . . and you are here now . . . while I am devastated. Help me to understand what it means for you to be with me and yet for me to feel this devastation.

I long for words of comfort, but now I can't hear them. Do you understand?

It can be difficult to get to the point of hoping on the other side of grief. The poet Emily Dickinson experienced a grief without much sense of hope, and wrote these beautiful lines:

> I measure every Grief I meet
> With narrow, probing, Eyes—
> I wonder if It weighs like Mine—
> Or has an Easier size.
>
> I wonder if They bore it long—
> Or did it just begin—
> I could not tell the Date of Mine—
> It feels so old a pain—

I wonder if it hurts to live—
And if They have to try—
And whether—could They choose between—
It would not be-to die—

I note that Some—gone patient long—
At length, renew their smile—
An imitation of a Light
That has so little Oil...

Still, we pray.

Give me hope, God.
Show me how to hope again.

HOPEFUL WORDS OF SCRIPTURE

God's loyal love couldn't have run out,

   his merciful love couldn't have dried up.

They're created new every morning.

   How great your faithfulness!

I'm sticking with GOD (I say it over and over).

   He's all I've got left.

   (LAMENTATIONS 3:22–24, MSG)

Be merciful to me, Lord, for I am in distress;
my eyes grow weak with sorrow,
my soul and body with grief.

(PSALM 31:9, NIV)

Do not let your hearts be troubled.

You believe in God; believe also in me. . . .

Peace I leave with you;

My peace I give you.

I do not give to you as the world gives.

(JOHN 14:1, 27, NIV)

The eyes of the Lord are on the righteous,

    and his ears are open to their cry.

The face of the Lord is against evildoers,

    to cut off the remembrance of them from the
earth.

When the righteous cry for help, the Lord hears,

    and rescues them from all their troubles.

The Lord is near to the brokenhearted,

    and saves the crushed in spirit.

(Psalm 34:15–18, nrsv)

I call to God;

   GOD will help me.

At dusk, dawn, and noon I sigh

   deep sighs—he hears, he rescues.

My life is well and whole, secure

   in the middle of danger

Even while thousands

   are lined up against me.

God hears it all, and from his judge's bench

   puts them in their place.

But, set in their ways, they won't change;

   they pay him no mind.

(PSALM 55:16–19, MSG)

I've told you all this so that trusting me,

you will be unshakable and assured,

deeply at peace.

In this godless world you will continue

to experience difficulties.

But take heart! I've conquered the world.

(JOHN 16:33, MSG)

Thomas Merton's Famous Prayer

My Lord God, I have no idea where I am going.

I do not see the road ahead of me.

I cannot know for certain where it will end.

Nor do I really know myself,

and the fact that I think I am following Your will

does not mean that I am actually doing so.

But I believe that the desire to please You

does in fact please you.

And I hope I have that desire in all that I am doing.

I hope that I will never do anything apart from that desire.

And I know that, if I do this, You will lead me by the right road,

though I may know nothing about it.

Therefore I will trust You always though

I may seem to be lost and in the shadow of death.

I will not fear, for You are ever with me,

and You will never leave me to face my perils alone.

The Ultimate Hope

For a Christian, there is a hope that can sustain us, to which we return in faith. This hope is found throughout the Scriptures, and in the liturgies of our churches.

O Lord, whose ways are beyond understanding,

listen to the prayers of your faithful people:

that those weighed down by grief

may find reassurance in your infinite goodness. . . .

Lord Jesus Christ,

by your own three days in the tomb,

you hallowed the graves of all who believe in you

and so made the grave a sign of hope

that promises resurrection

even as it claims our mortal bodies.

Grant that our

brother/sister/daughter/son/husband/wife, N,

may sleep here in peace

until you awaken *him/her* to glory,

for you are the resurrection and the life.

Then *he/she* will see you face-to-face

and in your light will see light

and know the splendor of God,

for you live and reign forever and ever.

O God,

by whose mercy the faithful departed find rest,

send your holy Angel to watch over this grave.

Through Christ our Lord.

(*From* "Prayers after Death,"
www.usccb.org; adapted)

Classic Words of Prayer–
But Only When You're Ready

A Prayer for Help at Night

I call upon you, O Lord; come quickly to me;
   give ear to my voice when I call to you.
Let my prayer be counted as incense before you,
   and the lifting up of my hands as an evening sacrifice.

(Psalm 141:1–2, NRSV)

A Prayer of St. Paul

Blessed be the God and Father of our Lord Jesus Christ,
the Father of mercies and the God of all consolation,
who consoles us in all our affliction, so that we may be
able to console those who are in any affliction with the
consolation with which we ourselves are consoled by God.

(2 Corinthians 1:3–4, nrsv)

THE PRAYER OF ST. FRANCIS

Lord, make me an instrument of your peace.

Where there is hatred, let me bring love.

Where there is offense, let me bring pardon.

Where there is discord, let me bring union.

Where there is error, let me bring truth.

Where there is doubt, let me bring faith.

Where there is despair, let me bring hope.

Where there is darkness, let me bring your light.

Where there is sadness, let me bring joy.

O Master, let me not seek as much

to be consoled as to console,

to be understood as to understand,

to be loved as to love,

for it is in giving that one receives,

it is in self-forgetting that one finds,

it is in pardoning that one is pardoned,

it is in dying that one is raised to eternal life.

THE PRAYER OF ST. PATRICK

I arise today

Through the strength of heaven;

Light of the sun,

Splendor of fire,

Speed of lightning,

Swiftness of the wind,

Depth of the sea,

Stability of the earth,

Firmness of the rock.

I arise today

Through God's strength to pilot me;

God's might to uphold me,

God's wisdom to guide me,

God's eye to look before me,

God's ear to hear me,

God's word to speak for me,

God's hand to guard me,

God's way to lie before me,

God's shield to protect me,

God's hosts to save me

Far and near,

Alone or in a multitude.

Christ shield me today

Against wounding.

Christ with me, Christ before me, Christ behind me,

Christ in me, Christ beneath me, Christ above me,

Christ on my right, Christ on my left,

Christ when I lie down, Christ when I sit down,

Christ in the heart of everyone who thinks of me,

Christ in the mouth of everyone who speaks of me,

Christ in the eye that sees me,

Christ in the ear that hears me.

I arise today through the mighty strength

Of the Lord of creation.

(ADAPTED)

FROM THE LITANY OF THE SAINTS

Kyrie eleison.
Lord, have mercy.

Christe eleison.
Christ, have mercy.

Kyrie eleison.
Lord, have mercy.

Holy Mary, Mother of God, pray for us.

Holy angels of God, pray for us.

All saints may be included here. Pray for us.

Lord, be merciful. Lord, save your people.

From all evil, Lord, save your people.

From every sin, Lord, save your people.

From Satan's power, Lord, save your people.

At the moment of death, Lord, save your people.

God of mercy,

hear our prayers and be merciful

to your *son/daughter N,*

whom you have called from this life.

Welcome *him/her* into the company of your saints,

in the kingdom of light and peace.

We ask this through Christ our Lord.

Amen.

(ADAPTED)

A Prayer of St. Elizabeth of the Trinity

During painful times, when you feel a terrible void, think how God is enlarging the capacity of your soul so that it can receive Him—making it, as it were, infinite as He is infinite.

Look upon each pain as a love-token coming directly from God in order to unite you to Him.

Call Out to God
Using One of God's Names

A prayer can often be a single word or phrase. The names for God carry so much meaning that sometimes all you have to do is say, call out, or simply whisper one of these names. . . .

Abba, Father (Galatians 4:6)

Savior (Acts 5:31)

Lord (1 Timothy 6:15)

Stronghold, Fortress (2 Samuel 22:3)

El Shaddai, "All-Sufficient One" (Genesis 17:1 and 28:3)

Shepherd (Psalm 23)

Emmanuel, God-with-Us (Matthew 1:23)

Peace (Judges 6:24 and John 16:33)

Ancient of Days (Isaiah 46:9–10)

All-Seeing God (Genesis 16:13)

Healing One (Psalm 6:2 and Luke 4:18)

The One Who Is There (Genesis 28:15 and Acts 7:48–49)

∽ UNVEILING ∽
A POEM BY RAMI SHAPIRO

*(In Jewish tradition it is customary to remove a veil covering
a new headstone at the first anniversary of a death.)*

In the eyes of eternity,

a thousand years are but a day,

our lives but a fleeting hour.

We arise to life,

as a wave cresting upon a vast and shoreless sea.

And we abandon life

as a wave abandons its shape

and returns to the source from which it swelled.

Arising, dissolving, returning yet never leaving

we are one with the eternal Source of Life now and forever.

The ragged tear death has rent in the fabric of our lives

cannot be mended.

Yet love is as strong as death;

and the bonds of love know no boundaries.

We still meet,

we still love;

if not in the world of physical reality

than in the gentler world of dream and memory.

The veil we remove

is but an outward sign

of an inner hiddenness.

When a loved one dies

there is often much fear

and anger and frustration and pain.

When a loved one dies we sometimes seek

to hide from the death

and veil ourselves from friends and memories.

But with this unveiling

we let go the hurt and fear,

we make peace with the living and the dead.

Out of respect for our loved

out of respect for our grief,

out of respect for our continuing obligations

to self and others,

to life and to community,

we remove the veil

and embrace the love

that so desperately wishes to envelop us.

From the Words of Scripture

He heals the brokenhearted

and binds up their wounds.

He determines the number of the stars

and calls them each by name.

Great is our Lord and mighty in power;

his understanding has no limit.

(Psalm 147:3–5, niv)

Then I saw a new heaven and a new earth; for the first
heaven and the first earth had passed away, and the sea
was no more. And I saw the holy city, the new Jerusalem,
coming down out of heaven from God, prepared as a bride
adorned for her husband. And I heard a loud voice from
the throne saying,

"See, the home of God is among mortals.
He will dwell with them;
they will be his peoples,
and God himself will be with them;
he will wipe every tear from their eyes.
Death will be no more;
mourning and crying and pain will be no more,
for the first things have passed away."

(Revelation 21:1–4, nrsv)

In the end, prayer's essence, its mission-statement, its deep raison d'être, is simply this: We need to open ourselves to God in such a way that we are capable of hearing God say to us, individually, "I love you!"

—RONALD ROLHEISER

INDEX